W9-AUS-073

THE BUILDING OF THE
TRANSCONTINENTAL RAILROAD

BY PEGGY CARAVANTES

Published by The Child's World®
1980 Lookout Drive • Mankato, MN 56003-1705
800-599-READ • www.childsworld.com

Photographs ©: akg-images/Newscom, cover, 1; Moses Swett/Library of Congress,
6; Everett Historical/Shutterstock Images, 8, 14, 25; Edward S. Curtis/Library of
Congress, 9; GL Archive/Alamy, 10; Library of Congress, 12; Red Line Editorial, 15,
24; Mathew Brady/War Department, 16; Alfred A. Hart/Library of Congress, 19, 20;
Alexander Gardner/Library of Congress, 22; Underwood Archives/UIG Universal
Images Group/Newscom, 26; A. and I. Kruk/Shutterstock Images, 28

ISBN 9781503816350
LCCN 2016945600

Printed in the United States of America
PA02370

ABOUT THE AUTHOR

Peggy Caravantes is an award-winning author of over 20 middle-grade
biographies and children's history books. She holds a bachelor of arts in
English and history as well as a master of education. A retired educator,
she currently enjoys tutoring elementary students. Caravantes is a PAL
(Published and Listed) member of the Society for Children's Book Writers
and Illustrators.

TABLE OF
CONTENTS

FAST FACTS

- Location: San Francisco, California, to Omaha, Nebraska
- Construction began: 1863
- Construction ended: 1869
- Cost: estimated $96 million to $111.5 million
- Length of railroad: 1,776 miles (2,858 km)
- Purpose: to connect the western and eastern parts of the United States with reliable transportation
- Materials: iron, wood
- Special features: Promontory Summit, Utah, was chosen as the joining place
- Engineers: Theodore Judah, Charles Crocker, James Strobridge, General Grenville Dodge, and Peter A. Dey

TIMELINE

1840s: Asa Whitney spends a decade and a fortune promoting the idea of a **transcontinental** railroad.

1849: Many people travel to California in search of gold.

1859: Theodore Judah appears before the U.S. Congress. He seeks funds to build a transcontinental railroad.

July 1, 1862: President Abraham Lincoln signs the Pacific Railroad Act.

January 8, 1863: Central Pacific breaks ground in Sacramento, California.

December 1863: Union Pacific breaks ground in Omaha, Nebraska.

1865: The U.S. Civil War ends.

1866: Union Pacific chief engineer Grenville Dodge hires workers for the east-to-west line.

April 28, 1869: Central Pacific lays 10 miles (16.1 km) of track in one day.

May 10, 1869: The two railroads are joined in a ceremony at Promontory Summit, Utah.

Chapter 1

UNITING A NATION

In the 1840s, Asa Whitney had a vision. He wanted a railroad to connect the eastern and western parts of the United States. Whitney was a good businessman. He believed a transcontinental railroad would help him make even more money. It would enable people and goods to move across the country more easily.

Whitney talked about his goal to anyone who would listen. He appeared before the U.S. Congress time and time again. The railroad would bring the country "together as one family," Whitney said.[1]

Much to Whitney's disappointment, Congress did not act. But Whitney was not ready to give up his dream. He went all over the United States. He laid out a plan showing how the railroad could pay for itself. The government could give the railroad a strip of land on either side of the track, Whitney said. Then the railroad could sell part of the land, the trees, and the minerals. The idea failed to get support. Whitney had spent a small fortune and had nothing to show for it. A defeated man, he gave up on his vision.

But the time was right for such a goal. In 1849, hundreds of thousands of people traveled to California in search of gold. Some of these people took long **stagecoach** trips. Others sailed south to Panama, crossed the jungle, and then sailed north to California. Still others sailed all the way around the tip of South America. A transcontinental railroad would make these slow, dangerous journeys unnecessary. It could provide a direct route across the entire United States.

▲ In the 1840s, voyages on passenger ships could take months.

People gathered in various cities to debate the issue. The one thing they did not discuss was Native Americans. No one talked about what a railroad would do to the Cheyenne and Sioux tribes that lived on the plains. Their lives depended on huge herds of bison. A railroad would prevent the animals from freely roaming the plains. The Native Americans' way of life would be destroyed.

Congress also ignored the Native American issue. They approved $150,000 to **survey** five possible routes for a transcontinental railroad. But the northern and southern states couldn't agree on one. The 1850s passed with no action taken. Would a transcontinental railroad ever be built?

▲ **Native Americans had lived in North America for thousands of years, long before European settlers arrived.**

Chapter 2

THEODORE JUDAH'S VISION

Theodore Judah, a young engineer from California, took up the fight. He had just supervised the building of the first railroad in California. It stretched from Sacramento to Folsom.

In 1859, 33-year-old Judah appeared before Congress. He said the transcontinental railroad was the "most magnificent project ever conceived."[2]

◀ **Many people referred to Theodore Judah as "Crazy Judah" because they thought his plan would never work.**

He believed the government should help pay for it. His ideas were interesting, and Congress listened to him. But they turned him down because the northern and southern states could not agree on the railroad's location. Judah did not give up. He said, "It is going to be built and I am going to have something to do with it."[3]

Judah returned to California. He began searching for people who would give him money for surveys. For his plan to work, he needed to find a way to cross the Sierra Nevada. This mountain range stretches across much of eastern California. Judah attracted four businessmen who became known as the Big Four. Along with Judah, they started a company called Central Pacific Railroad. The Big Four gave Judah money for his surveys.

Judah completed the surveys just before the U.S. Civil War began in 1861. The southern states had **seceded.** That meant they were no longer included in discussions about the railroad. There were no more objections to a northern route. Judah's hopes rose when Congress finally approved the Pacific Railroad Act in 1862. The act instructed two railroad companies to start laying track on opposite sides of the nation. The companies were called Central Pacific and Union Pacific.

Judah found the terms of the Pacific Railroad Act generous. The act gave the railroad companies land on which they could build the tracks. The act also paid them for each mile of track laid. The companies received more money for tracks going through mountains than for tracks on flat land. This made Judah happy. His railroad had to go through the Sierra Nevada.

Judah already knew the route he must follow. But he had no supplies or equipment. These all had to be brought from the East Coast. They had to travel around South America to San Francisco. There they were loaded on a steamer that took them up a river to Sacramento. Finally, after almost six months, Judah had the supplies he needed.

Workers broke ground on January 8, 1863, in Sacramento, California. But soon, Judah and the Big Four started disagreeing. Judah accused them of not including him in meetings. They told Judah he was spending more money than the plans called for.

Judah decided he needed new partners. He and his wife, Anna, set out for New York. But work on the transcontinental railroad had barely started. That meant the couple could not take a train across the country. So they boarded a ship and sailed south to Panama.

◀ **Hundreds of thousands of people died in the U.S. Civil War.**

▲ **One of the Big Four was Leland Stanford, who became the governor of California in January 1862.**

Then they made their way by train through Panama's mosquito-filled jungles. When they reached the Atlantic Ocean, they boarded another ship and sailed north.

▲ **Judah's journey from San Francisco to New York took weeks.**

Judah suffered from terrible headaches for several days. By the time he arrived in New York, Judah had a high fever that exhausted him. He could no longer walk. Several crew members carried him off the ship. He and Anna went to a hotel. Judah stayed in bed for an entire week. He got weaker and weaker.

Judah died in his wife's arms on November 2, 1863. Doctors said he had gotten yellow fever from a mosquito in Panama. Judah never got to see his dream fulfilled.

Chapter 3

PLANS DEVELOP, PROBLEMS BEGIN

In Omaha, Nebraska, General Grenville Dodge and Peter Dey made plans to build the Union Pacific's part of the transcontinental railroad. Their job was to supervise laying of the rail from east to west.

Other people were less concerned with railroads and more interested in making big money.

◄ **Durant worked as a doctor before he got involved in the railroad business.**

Dr. Thomas Durant bought $2 million worth of Union Pacific shares. This large purchase made him head of the company. But he was not satisfied. He believed he could make even more money in the actual building of the tracks.

Durant convinced other Union Pacific **investors** to form a company they called Crédit Mobilier. Union Pacific hired this company to build the eastern part of the transcontinental railroad. But it was a fake company, made up of Union Pacific investors.

Crédit Mobilier charged Union Pacific huge fees for labor and supplies. Union Pacific investors did not mind because the government was paying the bills. When Union Pacific received the money from the government, the investors paid Crédit Mobilier the actual costs. They kept the difference for themselves.

Durant and his investors cheated the government in other ways, too. They were being paid based on the number of miles of track completed. So they changed the route to make the railroad longer. That way, they got even more money. The actions of Crédit Mobilier became a huge scandal.

Union Pacific broke ground in Omaha, Nebraska, on December 2, 1863. But the company didn't lay much track at first.

There were not enough workers. The U.S. Civil War was still going on. Most young men were busy fighting. Finally, in 1865, the war ended. By early 1866, Dodge had hired Irish **immigrants** and former soldiers. But Union Pacific was already two years behind Central Pacific.

In California, the Central Pacific tracks had reached the Sierra Nevada. Now the railroad crews faced the difficult task of blasting tunnels through the hard granite of the mountains. The jobs were dangerous. Where would they find men brave enough to use explosives? Most of the white men in California were miners looking for gold. They had no interest in such hard work.

Charles Crocker, one of the Big Four, was chief of construction. He hired James Strobridge to supervise Central Pacific's workers. Crocker suggested that Strobridge hire some of the many Chinese men who lived in California. At first Strobridge refused. He did not believe Chinese workers were strong enough to do the work. He told Crocker, "I will not be responsible for the work done on the road by Chinese labor."[4]

Crocker reminded Strobridge that Chinese workers had done great things. "Hadn't they built the Chinese Wall?" Crocker asked.[5] By then, Strobridge was desperate. He agreed to give a few Chinese workers a try.

▲ **Each section of rail was 28 feet (8.5 m) long and weighed hundreds of pounds.**

The hard, dangerous work did not stop the Chinese. They handled explosions, avalanches, and freezing temperatures. At the work site, they worked in pairs.

▲ **A Chinese worker carries a load out of a tunnel.**

One worker lowered another in a basket down the steep face of the mountains. From the basket, the worker drilled holes into the rock, using only hand tools. Next he placed black powder in those holes. Then he lit the fuse, hoping he would be pulled up before the powder exploded.

Progress was slow. Sometimes workers moved the track forward only 1 foot (.3 m) per day. Some workers started sleeping in the tunnels at night. This saved time going in and out every day.

Strobridge had been wrong. The Chinese workers were doing a great job. Within a few years, 80 percent of the labor force was Chinese.

On the eastern side, Dodge finally had enough workers. He divided his men into teams. He told the surveyors to place wooden stakes. These showed the railroad's path. Next he told the graders to make the path smooth. The men struggled to move tons of dirt. They blew up any rocks they could not go around. They constructed bridges across bodies of water.

Tracklayers helped one another. They worked as two gangs of five men each. One gang stood on each side of the track. They strained to lift railroad **ties** into place. Next, workers placed the rails across the ties.

Finally, the spikers came. They pounded spikes through the rails and into the ties. This secured the rails in place. It took armies of workers to complete the backbreaking work. At one time, as many as 10,000 men worked on the Union Pacific rails.

Chapter 4

CHALLENGES

Workers for the Union Pacific often had too much spare time and too much money. Gun battles and bar fights were common. One newspaper reported, "Not a day passes but a dead body is found somewhere in the vicinity."[6] The worst report came out of Laramie, Wyoming. Five deaths and 15 injuries resulted from a gun battle there.

◀ **Building bridges was one of the most difficult parts of the project.**

Temporary towns sprang up as the crew of workers spread across the land. Few permanent buildings existed. Workers lived in tents or flimsy shacks. Company stores provided their basic needs. These wild towns moved with the workers as the rail construction advanced. Sometimes all they left behind were trash and mud chimneys.

As the railroad grew, workers continued to build on Native Americans' land. The Native Americans saw their land being taken over. They saw their source of food, the bison, being destroyed. Native Americans tried to protect their way of life.

In 1867, a group of Cheyenne warriors tried to derail a Union Pacific train. They removed a section of track. They also cut **telegraph** wires. A team of railroad workers did not know what had happened. They went to check out the situation. When the workers arrived at the damaged track, they were attacked. The Cheyenne killed four men. They injured another and left him for dead. Attacks such as this one caused many Americans to believe that Native Americans should be forced off their land.

The last few years of construction became a race between Union Pacific and Central Pacific workers. Both companies had increased their workforces.

MAP OF THE TRANSCONTINENTAL RAILROAD

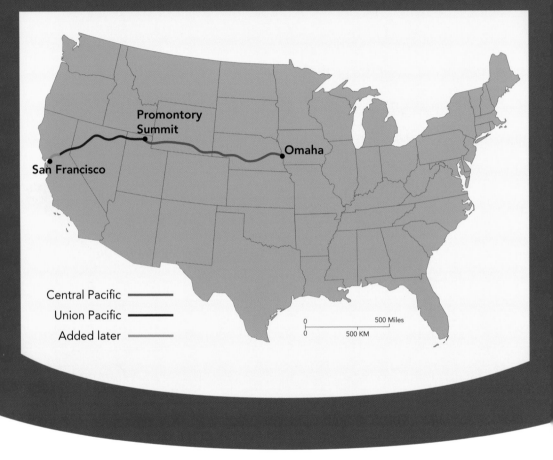

Central Pacific ————
Union Pacific ————
Added later ————

Promontory Summit

Omaha

San Francisco

0   500 Miles
0   500 KM

Each team was eager to show off its ability. On April 28, 1869, the Central Pacific crews laid 10 miles (16.1 km) of track in one day. An observer said, "it was like an army marching over the ground and leaving a track built behind them."[7]

By early May, the two sets of workers could see each other in the distance. Excitement grew as the workers waited to learn where the railroads would join. Officials for the railroads agreed on Promontory Summit in Utah.

▲ **Workers used horse-drawn carts to transport supplies.**

Chapter 5

SUCCESS!

The joining of the two railroads called for a ceremony. Officials from both companies took trains to the ceremony. They rode on tracks laid by their own workers.

At Promontory Summit, soldiers formed a double line on each side of the track. It was May 10, 1869. There were gold and silver spikes for the final linking of the two rails. Leland Stanford, one of the Big Four, stepped forward.

He lifted the heavy hammer and took a swing at a gold spike. But he missed! Workers yelled, "He missed it. Yee."[8]

Now it was Thomas Durant's turn. But his swing was no better than Stanford's. Workers yelled, "He missed it too, yow!"[9]

Workers removed the gold and silver spikes. They put regular iron spikes in place. Then they stepped up to drive the spikes through the rails. With mighty swings, they showed the bosses how it was done.

At last, the railroad was complete! A telegraph operator sent out a single word over the wires: "Done."[10]

This was a moment to remember forever. The Central Pacific Railroad had laid 690 miles (1,110 km) of track. The Union Pacific had completed 1,086 miles (1,748 km). Before the railroad had been built, the trip across the United States took six months and cost $1,000. Now it took less than a week and cost only $150.

The transcontinental railroad did more than just reduce the cost and travel time from one shore to the other. It provided a way for goods and mail to move faster. Today, trains carry approximately 40 percent of the goods Americans depend on. Lumber, steel, and food move on tracks across the United States.

But not all of the results of the railroad were positive. The railroad had a negative impact on the lives of Native Americans. New treaties with tribes gradually shrank their land holdings. Within a few decades, the government forced Native Americans onto **reservations**.

The transcontinental railroad represented the combined visions of a few men and the backbreaking work of thousands more. It was a major step in the United States' growth into a unified nation.

THINK ABOUT IT

- Do you think the railroad companies should have involved Native Americans in the planning process? Why or why not?
- James Strobridge did not think Chinese immigrants would make good workers. How were his stereotypes of Chinese workers different from reality?
- How might the railroad's route have been different if the southern states had not seceded?

◀ **Today, trains carry goods all across the United States.**

GLOSSARY

immigrants (IM-i-grunts): Immigrants are people who move from one country to another and settle there. Many Chinese immigrants helped build the railroad.

investors (in-VES-tuhrs): Investors are people who loan money to a company with the hope of getting more money back in the future. The Big Four were investors in the railroad.

reservations (rez-ur-VAY-shunz): Reservations are areas of land set aside by the government for a special purpose. The Native Americans were forced to live on reservations.

seceded (si-SEED-ed): Seceded means withdrew from another organization or government. The U.S. Civil War began after the South seceded from the Union.

stagecoach (STAYJ-koch): A stagecoach is a four-wheeled vehicle pulled by horses. In the 1800s, the stagecoach was used to carry people and mail.

survey (sur-VEY): Survey means to examine and measure land. Before building a railroad, people had to survey the land to figure out the best path.

telegraph (TEL-i-graf): A telegraph is an electric system for sending messages by a code over wires. The telegraph made long-distance communication very fast.

ties (TYZ): Ties are the pieces of wood that railroad tracks are built on. The workers put the ties into place and then put the metal tracks on top.

transcontinental (trans-kahn-tuh-NEN-tul): Transcontinental means going or extending across a continent. The transcontinental railroad went from Nebraska to California.

SOURCE NOTES

1. Christian Wolmar. *The Great Railroad Revolution: The History of Trains in America*. Philadelphia: Perseus, 2012. Print. 126.

2. George Kraus. *High Road to Promontory*. Palo Alto: American West, 1969. Print. 16.

3. David Haward Bain. *Empire Express: Building the First Transcontinental Railroad*. New York: Viking Penguin, 1999. Print. 62.

4. David Haward Bain. *Empire Express: Building the First Transcontinental Railroad*. New York: Viking Penguin, 1999. Print. 208.

5. George H. Douglas. *All Aboard!: The Railroad in American Life*. New York: Paragon House, 1992. Print. 120.

6. Stephen E. Ambrose. *Nothing Like It in the World: The Men Who Built the Transcontinental Railroad, 1863–1869*. New York: Simon & Schuster, 2000. Print. 218.

7. "Workers of the Central Pacific Railroad." *PBS*. PBS, n.d. Web. 26 May 2016.

8. Richard Scott, ed. *Eyewitness to the Old West: Firsthand Accounts of Exploration, Adventure, and Peril*. Lanham, MD: Roberts Rinehart, 2002. Print. 240.

9. Richard Scott, ed. *Eyewitness to the Old West: Firsthand Accounts of Exploration, Adventure, and Peril*. Lanham, MD: Roberts Rinehart, 2002. Print. 240.

10. "Golden Spike: Four Special Spikes." *National Park Service*. National Park Service, n.d. Web. 26 May 2016.

TO LEARN MORE

Books

Domnauer, Teresa. *Westward Expansion.* New York: Children's Press, 2010.

Friedman, Mel. *The California Gold Rush.* New York: Children's Press, 2010.

Perritano, John. *The Transcontinental Railroad.* New York: Children's Press, 2010.

Web Sites

Visit our Web site for links about the Transcontinental Railroad: childsworld.com/links

Note to Parents, Teachers, and Librarians: We routinely verify our Web links to make sure they are safe and active sites. So encourage your readers to check them out!

INDEX